Egg Watching

by Natalie Rompella
illustrated by Julia Noonan

PEARSON

Scott
Foresman

Editorial Offices: Glenview, Illinois • Parsippany, New Jersey • New York, New York
Sales Offices: Needham, Massachusetts • Duluth, Georgia • Glenview, Illinois
Coppell, Texas • Ontario, California • Mesa, Arizona

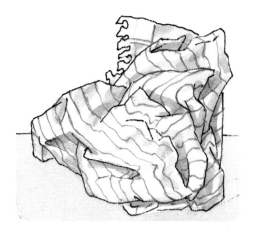

Melanie tore a sheet of paper out of her spiral notebook and crumpled it up. She was sitting in the backyard trying to write an outline for her science report, but she was out of ideas. She had tried writing about the greenhouse effect, the planets, and magnets, but she couldn't get into any of those topics. They were so boring! She needed something different, and she had to finish it before the week was over!

"Melanie," her mom called from the kitchen, "keep an eye on Tom while I make dinner. I don't want him in the treehouse by himself." Her little brother ran out the back door and up the treehouse ladder.

"But Mom, I am trying to get my work done," protested Melanie.

"Just do me this favor for a few minutes," her mother said in an authoritative tone.

Melanie rolled her eyes. She picked up her notebook and headed for the treehouse.

"Melanie, Melanie, Melanie!" Tom shouted from the treehouse. She knew he wouldn't be quiet until she answered him.

"What, Tom?" she asked as she climbed the ladder.

"I found bird eggs! Come and see!"

Melanie sighed. *Well, I'm not getting anywhere on this outline,* she thought. *I might as well see what he's yelling about.*

Tom pointed out three tiny eggs tucked away in a nest made of straw and twigs. Tom was excited, but Melanie didn't see what the big deal was.

"I think they're robin eggs," he said.

"How do you know?" Melanie asked.

"My teacher says that robin eggs are light blue, just like those," Tom answered, eager to show off what he had learned in school.

"Melanie, Tom," their mom called out to them from the doorway of the house. "Time to come in for dinner."

"What are we having?" Melanie called back.

"Roast beef and carrots," her mother said.

Melanie made a face at her brother. She didn't like roast beef or carrots. If she had her choice, she would eat pizza every night for dinner. Tom made a face too.

"Why do we have to have carrots?" Melanie whined. She opened the pot of carrots simmering on the stove and wrinkled her nose.

"They're good for you! They'll make your hair curly and your cheeks rosy," her father joked as he came in the room. He was always trying to be funny.

During dinner, Tom couldn't stop talking about the robin eggs.

"When do you think they'll hatch?" asked Tom.

"I don't know," said Melanie. She wasn't really listening to him. As she poked at the nub of a carrot, she thought about her science project.

"I didn't see the mother. Maybe we should keep an eye on them."

"Sure, whatever," replied Melanie.

* * * *

The next morning, Tom crashed into Melanie's room. "Let's go check the eggs!"

"What eggs?" Melanie asked drowsily. "Oh right. Can't I just sleep a little longer?"

Tom shook his head vigorously. "You promised!"

"OK, OK," said Melanie. "Just give me a minute."

As they left the house, their father caught up to them. "Don't forget to wear a sweatshirt. It's cold outside."

"But it's spring," Melanie complained.

"It's still chilly," her dad replied.

Reluctantly, Melanie and Tom both put on sweatshirts and headed to the treehouse to check on the eggs.

Tom had checked on them three times the day before and had not seen the mother robin. But she must have been there. The eggs looked as if they had been rearranged.

"I hope we see the mother bird today. The eggs could hatch any day now," said Tom.

"There she is!" Melanie pointed to the mother robin as she flew up to the nest and settled on the eggs.

"What is she doing?" asked Tom.

"She's sitting on them to keep them warm. Maybe they'll hatch soon."

On Wednesday three baby birds were chirping loudly right outside the treehouse window. Melanie and Tom got their parents to come up for a better look. They all watched the small birds. Each one had wrinkly skin and only a few downy feathers. They lay curled up in the bottom of the nest.

"They are so small," Tom said.

"They must have just hatched," their mom commented. "Why don't we give them some privacy for a couple of days? Then we can check on them again."

Three days later, the weather had become warmer, and there were four birds in the nest now. They were bigger, and soft down feathers had grown on their bodies. They were all sitting up and snuggling together. Each one looked up at the sky and chirped loudly.

"What are they doing?" asked Tom, watching the baby birds with their beaks pointing up.

"They are waiting for the mother bird to bring them food," explained their father. "She's probably out hunting for some now."

"What if she doesn't come back?" Tom asked, worried.

"She will," their mother answered. "She knows her babies are waiting for her."

After watching for a while, their parents left. Melanie and Tom waited for the mother bird for a little while longer. They stared out the window for half an hour. The babies just kept their beaks up in the air, waiting.

Melanie grew impatient. She really needed to get back to her science project.

"Let's go, Tom. She's not coming right now."

"Maybe we should do something," Tom said.

"What could *we* do?" asked Melanie.

"We could bring them some food," suggested Tom.

"Well, let's ask Mom before we do anything."

They found their mom working at the computer.

"Mom," began Tom, "the birds' mother still hasn't come back to the nest. What should we do?"

"What do you think you should do?" she asked. "They are wild animals, after all. I'm afraid anything you might do to help will just hurt them."

"But what if we brought them some food?" asked Melanie. She was beginning to worry about the birds too. "They could have some of the leftover carrots."

Mom shook her head. "Robins eat worms."

"Wow!" said Melanie. "And I thought we had to eat some awful stuff!"

Her mother smirked. "Very funny, Melanie."

"Well, we could bring them to the vet," said Tom. "I bet it wouldn't hurt for them to have a checkup."

"They don't need a checkup like pets do," said their mother. "The car ride over would only frighten them."

"Are you sure there is nothing we can do?" asked Tom. He was still set on bringing food out to the birds.

"Just let them be. Their mother will take care of them."

Tom and Melanie looked at each other. "Well, we're going to sit outside and watch them, just in case," said Tom.

"We are?" Melanie turned to her brother.

"Come on, Melanie. You know I can't go in the treehouse alone!"

"But I have work to do!"

"Just go with your brother for a while," their mother interrupted. "You can do your work up there."

Melanie looked at her brother's determined face. "Oh, all right! But I'd better be able to get some work done on my science report!"

Melanie followed Tom back outside to the treehouse.

"I still think we should do something," said Tom.

"Mom said they're OK. Just leave them alone," said Melanie.

Tom ignored his sister. "We could feed them worms."

"And just where are we going to find worms?" asked Melanie.

"Well, there must be some in the backyard somewhere. They live in the dirt," said Tom. He was very proud of himself for coming up with such a logical idea.

"We need something to collect them in."

Tom had a solution for that too. "I bet there's something up in the treehouse we can use."

Melanie looked around the treehouse. There were many different odds and ends. An old teddy bear sat on a card table, some books were stacked in the corner, and a pillowcase was draped over a dusty, old dollhouse.

She picked up the tattered pillowcase. Their father had used it last summer to catch a speckled rattlesnake. Surely it would hold worms.

"We could use this!" she said triumphantly, and slung the pillowcase over her shoulder. She had suddenly forgotten about her homework.

Melanie and Tom got to work looking for worms. Neither of them had much luck. Tom looked under rocks and near the sandbox. He found an anthill and a roly-poly bug that curled into a ball when he touched it. Melanie thought she saw a brownish-colored worm but, lunging closer, realized it was only a small twig. She poked her finger in the soil by the roses but didn't find anything there, either.

Back in the treehouse, they both sat down in front of the window again and stared out at the birds. Their beaks were up, searching for the food their mother was supposed to bring.

Tom sighed and laid back on the floor. "I can't watch anymore. It's getting boring."

"Maybe Mom's right." Melanie said. "Maybe the mother will come back."

"Yeah," agreed Tom. "Maybe she has been coming when we aren't here to see her."

"Let's just forget about it for a while. I need to work on my science report, anyway." Melanie got up from the window and curled up in the corner with her pencil and paper. She began writing out ideas again.

Tom lay on the floor a little while longer. Then he got up and began pacing around the treehouse.

"I'm bored," he said. "Will you play a game with me?"

Melanie put down her notebook again. "I might as well. I still can't think of a topic for my science report."

Tom got out the box of checkers, and they began to set up the pieces.

Melanie sighed, moving one of her checkers. "No luck feeding the baby birds. And I still have to find a topic for my science report."

A couple of minutes later, Melanie caught a glimpse of something near the treehouse window.

"Look!" Melanie pointed to the nest. The mother robin was perched next to it. She flew down to the ground and began pecking. She fluttered from one spot to another, prodding at the ground. After a while, they saw her pull what looked like a long string from the grass.

"A worm!" Tom gasped. "How did she do that? I looked there, but I didn't find any."

The two crept over to the window as the mother robin flew back up. As she landed on the side of the nest, the babies' chirps became louder. They began opening and closing their mouths. Melanie and Tom watched the mother feed one of her babies.

The mother robin dropped the worm into the mouth of the baby that was the most rowdy. Then she flew away.

"How come that one is the only one that gets to eat?" Tom asked.

"She'll come back." They waited, but she didn't come back.

"Why does she take so long to feed her babies?" asked Tom.

"Maybe it's hard finding worms," Melanie said. "At least she's feeding them something."

Just then, the children heard their mother calling from the house. Melanie started down the treehouse ladder, followed by Tom.

As they headed back to the house, they saw the mother robin poking in the grass near the flower bed. She pulled another worm from the ground and flew back toward the nest with the worm wiggling in her mouth.

"Hey!" said Melanie, as she pointed to the flowers. "I looked in that spot! There weren't any worms there before."

They looked up at the tree. The mother bird was perched near the nest again, feeding the worm to her babies.

"I'm going to watch from the treehouse again," Tom said, romping toward the ladder. As he got closer to the nest, the mother robin dropped the worm in the nest and flew away. Once again, she had not finished feeding all of her babies.

Tom stopped running and looked up at the nest. It was clear how disappointed he was that the robin flew away again.

That's when Melanie got an idea.

"Tom, come back over here!" Melanie called to him. He ran back. "What?"

"I think I know why we don't see the mother very much. She always waits until we are out of sight."

"Why?" Tom looked puzzled.

"I think she is protecting her babies. She didn't want us to see where she had hidden her nest."

Their dad came out with binoculars. "I thought maybe you two could use these." He handed them to Tom, who focused on the nest. "The mother robin is back. And there's another bird!"

"Let me see," Melanie said.

"That's probably the father. I've been looking up robins on the Internet. The babies need a lot of food," their dad began. "The father helps find food and feeds them."

"Do they eat only worms?" asked Tom.

"Good question," their father answered. "We could look that up too."

"Hey, I just thought of a good topic for my science report: robins!" exclaimed Melanie.

"That sounds like a good idea," their dad said. He started walking toward the house. "Now you two need to wash up for lunch. I made you tuna sandwiches."

"Being a mother bird is hard work," Tom said to Melanie. "You have to fly around finding worms in the grass, protect your baby birds from enemies, and keep them warm."

"Yeah," said Melanie, trying to remember everything she had seen for her science report.

"Lunchtime," called their mom from the kitchen window.

"Kind of like Mom and Dad do for us, right?" said Melanie.

They smiled and went in for lunch.

Robins

The American robin is a very common type of bird in the United States. It is usually found in the eastern part of the country. In early spring, robins appear in the Northeast. They are one of the very first signs of the seasons' change. In the fall, they fly to the Southeast, where they spend the winter.

You can recognize a robin by the red feathers on its chest. The first settlers named the bird *robin* because it reminded them of a bird with similar coloring in England. This bird is called the European robin.

A mother robin will make her nest high in the trees or on the ledges of buildings. During the year, a mother will take care of two or three different groups of babies. While the mother keeps the eggs warm, the father will bring worms, insects, fruits, and berries back to the nest to eat. When the eggs hatch, both the mother and father feed and protect the babies.